The Devil's Troubadour

a compendium of poetical works

by

Count MoriVond

Bloomington, IN  Milton Keynes, UK

authorHOUSE®

AuthorHouse™
1663 Liberty Drive, Suite 200
Bloomington, IN 47403
www.authorhouse.com
Phone: 1-800-839-8640

AuthorHouse™ UK Ltd.
500 Avebury Boulevard
Central Milton Keynes, MK9 2BE
www.authorhouse.co.uk
Phone: 08001974150

First published by AuthorHouse 9/10/2007

ISBN: 978-1-4259-4682-1 (sc)
ISBN: 978-1-4259-5179-5 (hc)

Printed in the United States of America
Bloomington, Indiana

This book is printed on acid-free paper.

Disclaimer:

THIS IS FANTASY

...infuse the puerile minds with the tales of Parisian Decadents, with Bacchic reenactments in the silken boudoir. The under-aged pucker to the sedative and condemn their hapless souls to the auburn chiffon

the

Devil's

Troubadour

A COMPENDIUM
OF POETICAL WORKS

CONTENTS

the Scribe

Scribe of iniquities wrought
From thy quill a feast for the wicked
Whose lyric stake the faith-filled heart,
Impaling the insipid of spirit
Entreat my unearthly summons
Beith as ever, unparalleled in thy lusts
Sack the restraint and urge to err
Thy most decadent work, I commission and entrust
Nocuous bard, lyrical fiend
Evil seethes through thy balmy psalm
Pursue the heralding, tempestuous qualm
That the chaos of night pays laughter

the
Devil's
Troubadour

1877

Afloat an Opus
of Scarlet Gluttony

Parlaying about these rings of poverty
Cloistered in the folds of the godless
Unto ye my beloved, house of ill repute
Where my loathsome wants are given solace
Music-maker, rend her mantra upon my arrival;
The pornographers psalm, the masochists grate
Andante, allegretto, in shackles they wait
From gagged and bound, to pronged and barbed
Prey, in its leathered grace
Afloat an opus of scarlet gluttony
Into the house of Satan's fane

Undulating lusts permeate her strident scent
Appetites wetted in the urge of impropriety
Enter the wenches and rollicking rogues
With loose and supple bosoms heaving
What obscene voluptuousness, dancing in violence
Perspiring heaven, gyrating bliss
Eucharist areolas in communions of licentious silence
Bordello of affection, shelter me in thy midst
Afloat an opus of scarlet gluttony
God forlorn, for earthly bliss

A strange whimsicality
The strings lived
The horns in awe, silent
Granting the keys to give
With soft percussion pulsates
This sweet miasma of sound
Sent to free us from our frivolity
Rousing the profound
Cohesion like no other
Upon this midnight lark
To what divinity do I owe thee?
Ye, gracious things impart;

This beauteous music emancipates
From Day's monotonous grange
And rends us purely ingratiated,
Into the wondrous and estranged...

'Her bulbous arce entrenched in my fornication
Imploring the intercession of a divine messenger
Whirling up her lather. Lost in lusts elation
I've penetrated my member into the most, unmemorable
of ventures
But ye my lost Christine, I ought surely thee,
remember'

Christine

How I long this fresh beatitude
A flower named Christine
My affections rub her ruddy
Blushingly pristine

"I will instruct you in these ways
Christine, do not be tame."
Disrobed, falls her satin dress
As does her face in shame

The pale nubile flesh
Plump to my heart's content
Crossed shy, her luscious legs
"I can smell you getting wet."

To tongue this rosebud un-bloomed
To lap the pink of its sweet flavor
For purity goads this un-implorable doom
To despoil thee of grace and favor

…As the Devil to indulge, my dear
In the fruits of God's labor;
A flower called Christine
An urge I shall not waiver

Ah this fresh beatitude,
A flower named Christine
To tongue this rosebud un-bloomed
T'was to savor the last of chastity

And in the vapors of her musky furring,
Of her ever gaping pudendum
I am all too soon burying
My snout with ravenous momentum

And her vulva athrust, a twitching wink
Cooing in her velvet strokes
Elation on the brink
Of the plunging tongue that laps and pokes

And the taste of her femininity
Salinity, sweet, sublime
Like Dionysian wine, the blood of Christ
The elixir of those divine

How I long this fresh beatitude
A morsel named Christine
Condemned I am to appetence
And seldom dear, relieved

the Incubus

Insatiably pressed for wantonness
Smote, parched and hungrily vexed
This scorcher desire floods my cavernous vessels
To my greatest erection yet
Like a vile protruding, brooding eel
Seething with larcenous intent
To steal the un-ploughed of innocence
To defile and forge entrance,
This most vilest eel, so virile and malevolent
Seeking to seize the unsullied, immaculate
To release from puritan tethers
And condemn to graver duress

As thus did one, as if from heaven descended
Ingenuously frivolous 'though in cleanliness kept
To poison my sleep, to pound in my head
Oh bedlam of all obsessions!
With a face of purest angel
Shied behind a tress of golden silk
Starry eyes of childish blue
Skin of pearls, of cloud, of milk
And there my member firmed
With Herculean vigor and mass irascible pent
To seize this dame in her untouched allure
Before her innocence is cleft

In youths gait she goes, in careless promenade
Unknowing of the fates to encounter
A perilous journey through a prettiest jaunt

Through a path of laments, shall she wander
Into my garden of dreams, wherein I lay at unrest
You stroll unbeknownst of this iniquity
Upon the breeze I assail my lusted behest
To reinvent in thy soul, servility

For I am as the demon of careless dreaming
The eater of souls, when the flesh is at rest
The infanticide in deflowering
The adult tears of youth's regrets
Submerged in the fires of my hunger
Athirst for my purge; insidious
Needling with merited loathing
Hell is stoked; this blissful oblivion

...predation elates

Eyes of Serpents

Mass of the serpent
Eve of the end
Sadist, the servant
The mass will begin

(The serpent said…)

"Snake eye blind
Never to shut
Cursed to slither
When once I walked
Tempt the virgins
I'll eat her fruit
Bleeding orgy
Piercing maroon
Ancient day
The coming of reptile
Orgasming, choking
Filling the Nile
I am snake
I seduce with fear
I slide in cunt
I ruleth here."

These Divine Songs

Tongued the entrance
Of my kingdom
Danced enchanted
As she gazed in famine
Swoons of decadence
Impeccable decadence
Its raw wet scent
Welcoming to pleasantries

Face gently brushed
In her tangled grove
A gaze of splendor
As glistened lips are clove
I wander her halls
To supernal moans
May these divine songs
Reach celestial throes

Can you hear my ancient love,
Reach the highest note?
Blithest ripples transcend into dance
Orchestrating mysteries below

Heaven is pink, wet and welcoming

Ambrosia of Cunts

The nectar of thy saccharine cleft
Has ebbed thy wanton toxin
Luring to thy pasty flesh
Pale and soft as cotton
Of all but venom thou art bereft
Malice vassal; a soul's calamity
How I must long for the poisonous
Consumed, engulfed, indefinitely
Clitoral proclivities,
Lascivious appetites
How such exude, the loins of ferity
Baiting me to bite...
The pouty lips that curve and whist
That wetted "mouth" that'd open for me
Those hearty thighs that press without rest
Are cruel as they deny me
The savor of that pink, my heart's duress
Crueler still, they that bind me
As I've mine reveries of yearning flesh
All the time, every time, to haunt me
Those heartless fists, that wills resist
Knows not the weight of my longing
Those hearty hips that thrust and whip
Will tend to but one in the morning
For then I am off to duly fill
The void wrought o' my yearning despair...
And the voids of many a damsel
Amply endowed and proud as they bare
The slick glint of their pink amore
Etiquette destitute but bugger like hares

And bugger I shall, these buxom whores
Until I'm too drunk to care
'Pon the nectar of those saccharine clefts
That ebb my wanton toxin
That lures me to their pasty flesh
Pale and soft as cotton
Of all but venom thou art all bereft
Malice vassals; a soul's calamity!
How I must long for the poisonous
Consumed, engulfed, indefinitely

- For riches yet claimed, by minds or hands
In pleasures own pursuit
In which we may, all things eschew
That speak of vile necessity...

I will exult my throne among the stars,
The cenotaphs of antique fiefdom
And the monoliths of ancient Gods

- And bring darkness unto light

- And dance among the fearful

...Give yourself to words
And humor me, my dear
That your subconscious filters in
The subliminals that I rear
Whilst that state of "rapid eye"
I will patiently await
To insert my terse suggestions,
The transgressions I've for bait

Red Rubenesque

My buxom "Ruben's", I could not resist
The deficiency in pigmentation, and the thickness of the hips
Slothful un-worked hands and pale lily feet
With scarlet tress and satin sheets, inebriated in vanity

Be plushed as the clouds, billowing and sweet
Ever opened to my persuasions, however perverse, the deed
Lay sprawled and idle be, resistless and welcome me
To the confection between your thighs, to that ever
delectable treat

Through her vaporous and wetted mesh
A succulent plum exudes its scent
An un-plucked rose, un-bloomed and kept
In the sanctity of cleanliness, my sanctums nest

A burning bush of red pubescence,
An effluvia – mellifluous!
Of glistened labium and unsheathing hood
With exuberance twitched and with radiance stood
As if demanding at once her deflowering
And efflorescence into womanhood

Legs o'er her head, a hand upon her mouth
Eyes, from desire to untimely dread
As I point my poniard deep down south

Deep down the vestal,
Venus mound. Into the holy land
I pummel with rage that delicate surrender

Muffling wails with my hand
Through glorious spurts of crimson splendor
To pass, innocence I render,
Gaping you, so tender...for animal, I am

The guttural disgorge of purity,
Purged from their virgin throats
A music like no mirthful melody,
A brilliant succession of notes

Past the crimson aperture
Purged from its bloodied maw
She delivers her exhortation
Menstrual gush and fertile thaw

…And all the bottles are empty,
All the whores are spoken for

What enormous conviction in spontaneity;
To be primal, and now and nothing more.

Jezreel and Esdraelon

Celestial sphere at dusk
Envelop the sovereign minds
Embower and helm as thus
Diadem for those divine

As the skylark, we've resulted
Monarchs of the clouds
Upon wispy wings exulted
Unto vast flight's whereabouts

Now let us be as children
And forget for which we strive
But BE, in self-negligence
And springs of scampering lithe

Now let us be as beasts
Without care or consequence
Intuitively free to feast
For our natures recompense

A poem to proselytize
The stars to our mutiny
Dissension parts thee, vaulted sky
Carefree beneath "God's" scrutiny

And wearing the gleaming nimbus;
Diadem for those divine
For WE live pure, as child and beast;
The jewels that ever shine

(and soon the zephyr would whisper...)

I am the prince jeweled hand
    On your Left-hand Path
A fanged serpent kiss
    Of pagan salts and ancient bliss
Of palpitating ardors
     On lascivious tongues
     And incestuous lips
Undulating, ubiquitous
     And so solicitous...

I am the Prince jeweled hand
    Of deliverance...

The imaginable becomes tangible
And the surreal, made to order
Obsess here now the unattainable.
The supernals aerate, support her
Polymorphous marveled skies,
Like a spirit begging for corporeity
For blessed night is the revenant.
Unfolding and offering, satiety

Blessings

Blessed art thou truly
The maidens' young and fair
Whom dance their drunken bliss's
Romanced without a care

Blessed thou art duly
A festive treat of the wild
Loving me like an animal
Holding me like a child

And a fortnight's score of yonder whores
Of wantonness imbed
To lovers of lust, vice and wine
To you alone, I'm wed

For my love subsists in brothel trysts
Of tender affections appointed
Where with closed eyes and opened legs
Lay the amicably exploited

Blessed art thou truly
The maidens' young and fair
Whom dance their drunken bliss's
Romanced without a care

Blessed art thou truly
Whom assuage the savage heart
Who release the rod from yearning
With lips where lusts impart

"I descended from heaven
One Godless night
And whored myself sore,
And succored in much wine
And murdered and raped
And plundered and reigned
For born of the divine
I am allowed the mundane"

Asmodeus

I am the daemon of lust
Asmodeus, be the name
I make the Goddesses blush
As I entice with pleasures profane

I am the root of fornication
In every form and famed contention
The muse for lovers, both pure and vile
In every salacious expression

With my profligate propensities
And fetishistic penchants
I make the trembles ease
And allow no apprehension

When the libidinous insists
Bearing riddance of control
'Tis I whom make all cease their resist
And bear what I unfold

Yes, the root of fornication
Ever luring and ever so quaint
To rend void that final bastion
Of puritan restraint

The demon, soliciting sinners
To transcend the transgressed
By the mercurial obscenities
I call now to manifest

For as when my fingers snap
The pheromones release
Making maidens affordable wenches
Bringing kings to their knees

And as I stroke my horns
All present members erect
And as I wag my filthy tail
Their queen wives undress

Ah, the orgiastic copulations
Are my manifold creations
A coital cornucopia of elations
And swooned debauchery

So malcontent and mischievous
Unrepentant and insidious
Lewd and in lust, lascivious
In every discrepancy

I am the daemon of lust
Asmodeus be the name
In every lick and every thrust
In everyone who ever came

In the psyche of ye all, firmly am I cemented
And as I cannot be exorcised, I will not be rejected…

Green Fairy

A little anise, licorice, hyssop and veronica
The green fairy, in the emerald glass stood
Fennel, lemon balm, sugar and angelica
And lots of that wormwood, oh wondrous wormwood
And into the forest, where their wanders deemed
Dancing to a song that few fellow ears hear
T'ward glowing bonfires the fairy did lead
Where many nude witches and satyrs appeared
Shall Sylvanus dance? Would Faun, would mischievous Pan?
Playing his lyre to her forest nude frolics
In ecstasies fumbling, through asphodels and lilacs
Will the priestess now warm, to a full moon romanced?
Would Sylvanus, would Faun, would mischievous Pan?

Stygian Procession

…Satyrs of profane joy
Who betongue the suffering, with jocund blithe
Mocking those in woe, who kneel in supplications
Rejoiced before those, who in torments writhe
To brace their visage, is to court impending plague
Trespassing the beds of immaculate rest
Disheveled in their bleeding, lay their plethora of game;
Deflowered promises of long lusting repress

Satyrs of profane joy
Who scour in ceaseless prowl, to debauch an animal crave
Mad cackles haunt the paths where lay predations sated remains
To brace their visage alone, is to prelude thy fall from grace
To revel in the inimical, with witches fowl and fey
Excursion her now, this true Elysium
Where the satyrs promenade
Forests behind twilights divine
Wilderness through sin and slay

Perusing the musings of one Nicholas Drake
Far from melancholy but for melancholy's sake
I pondered the fragile human satire;
The tragicomedy prior my wake:

Orchids of Polio

Hearken clouds, a passing grace
Pillowed my thoughts to indolence
Embroiled aloft, it's capricious whim
Billowing with calm and patience

Then, the firmament seizes me, in total captivation
What austere grandness, what vague sublimity
As slowly I succumb to my infantile paralysis
Night, veil the muted scream to a silenced serenity

Night, en-soul the vapid sighing
A sun bewails a fortnights spent
On the miseries I have pent
A sun forbidding the moon's ascent

Night, deprive me not the idleness
In the winces of tiny words
And in breezed her tranquil halcyon,
Her clarion call o'er hyacinth walls

-A covenant of her reprisal
New colours and Aesopian words
In whispered her tranquil halcyon
Amidst the clouds of hovering herds

Night, reprieve me not my detriments
For character, such bestow
I do not mourn my heart's content
But strengthen the weak of woe

Night, illumine there my dissonance
Paralyzed and restrained
Tethered to this immobile silence
I offer you my pain

…And she stifles my trembling quill
To grant me the gift of motion
Night, I shall and forever will
Service thee, with fealty's devotion

"The sky is overcast
With concerts of the celestial
Empyrean ringing splendid
Wind chimes of tinsel crystal
Propounding from their fathoms
Its lissome gist of starry bright
Tonight, the eventide was the "aria"
Prelud'ing "nocturne's" flight
Oh subconscious wanderlust
In thy midnight vellum, enrapt
Through vastest darkling, I am thrust
Through velvet veils of black
In quietus, introspection
'Tis here that I shall know me
But my silence portends omens
Solemn and unholy"...

Perfidies, the Wraith

Once upon a time, of women and wine
And vials of assorted vices
Once betwixt the interval blackouts
And artificial paradises,
He mired marooned in dissonance
With introspection and threnody
As the abstract of reflection uncoiled
In disturbing familiarity;

(a sensual epiphany sojourned into his dreams)

A serpent named Perfidies
With teeth as blades, unsheathed to release
A sinister grin, through-
Which 'evil' seethes
A starved gnarl and cusped gnash
Depthless orbs of scrying black glass
Whose gaze was phantasmagoria,
Exploration and mystery,
Gnomic riddles in bucolic verses
And a lyric called prophecy

With an encircling slither
And trenchant jaw agape
Drew closer this epiphany
Who in unknown tongue spake:

"the empirical is subliminal
in every observation
the obvious will obviate

beyond all speculation.

subterfuge is sovereign
when rationale submits to fancy
faith precludes all sentience
and answers always nothing

turner of stones,
prier of dusted vaults
you've a curious will,
without default
whom dost not ever,
blindly believe
thus dare I'd never,
ye deceive
yet however resolute
in thine conviction
thou must never forget
that all is perception
for what are truths to you,
may be lies to me
as all is dependent
upon how one perceives"

He pondered his death
In those eyes of obsidian
From dusk and dawn
And into the meridian
'Til his iridescence was consumed
In it's obese silhouette
Abomination of Sidonia
Countenance of atonement
And the serpent said:

"mine is the work of religion
to coerce to idle bondage
the works of faith and holy fiction
are my tyrannies in progress
all distinct and intrinsic
and flawlessly there woven
brainwashed are the bleating sheep
by the shepherds I have chosen"

Faith, now ever breached
Erodes in burning lumber
The fates had wrought her cumber;
O' Perfidies, the wraith
In flames, caress the wonders
The crosses and faithful numbers
The souls, from lies asunder
Imperiled and in pain
And the spirits wake destitute
Bewailing in deep despondency
Clemencies squeal their pealing
In exasperating pleas,
Supplicating for salvation

Where there could never be
The myth of God, the breath of faith
Vanquished eternally.

Our Father'; Autolatry

Our Father who art – dead!
Hallowed be, thine diligence bled
- Your kingdom is dumb
- Muted and numb
Your apostles in apostasy fled

Give us this day, our daily deception
Carrion of Christ in cordial reception
- No communal wine,
- Nor confessional line
Will lead us to our redemption

Now let me tell you of an irony
Of a messiah employed in carpentry
- A joke of godhood
- Nailed, to two pieces of wood
Reinforcing my autolatry

Is this the grace of God divine?
A corpse, on a tree? – I must decline
- For a martyrs mantel-shelf
- As you could not save yourself
You died for YOUR sins… not mine

This "king" in incompetence drowned
Less of God and more of clown
- Divine salvation?
- For failure's coronation…
Bloodied brow and hawthorn crown

Sex without violence…how oddly novel.

The Sadist's Plate:

A LOVERS TALE OF CONSENSUAL TORTURE

Like a maniacal senility
Threatening to manifest
There is criminal liability
In every impetus
The adrenaline of lust enrapts
Still, enflamed and vicious
Like petrified as stone it is
And fortified with malice
And these terrible hands prolong the bliss
The push, the stretch of ecstasies fist
There is no pleasure, no summit to this
But to glut upon, thine anguish
And the perpetual thrust that marauds you numb
Will persist beyond what ought to be
To the terror filled sibilant shrill
Bewailing odes of sodomy
Bestializing my soul, her screams
En-lusting my heart with savagery
Lie upon the sadist's plate
And know that love is agony

Lay ye here thy torments
Flow 'til overflowing
You will bleed forth my libations
And assuage my every longing
You will bleed 'til you are dormant
Ebbing the price of redemption

Engulf Hell's wanton gullet
With sacrifice and adoration

To love me is to drudge and scrape
To lie upon the sadist's plate
To open thy legs and welcome pain
To know my love is hate
For my grip holds strong with tightening tight
Biting your thighs with remorseless might
Spitting your face whilst you now lick my boots
Pulling your hair, from bloodied roots
How I indeed, love thee simply,
Or simply love to beat thee?
Upon fealty's empurpled knees
Oh Lords, I delight in cruelty!

So lay ye here, thy torments
And flow 'til overflowing
Bleeding ceaselessly, my libations
Assuaging my every longing
You will bleed 'til you are dormant
Ebbing the price of redemption
Engulf Hell's wanton gullet
With sacrifice and adoration

By manacles, shackles and chains
All forthright unholy tethers
Fettered rope and rolls of tape
The terror-awed drenched leathers
Endure it all and thou may endear
This love, this drudge and scrape
I kiss with bite, I love with rape
Upon my sadist's plate

...The carotid pulse pinched and pressed

To breathless incognizance and ephemeral death

Lacunae

Awaken from slumbers thrall
My pretty one, my darling pretty
Arise to Night's call…
Come, you are ready
For a feast of life, a garden of hope
Where the nightingales are singing
We've come to take you by the hand
Do you feel your instincts ringing?

Delicate ears prostrated before
The euphony that seeps from the pores
Percolate they, through astral threads
The scales of grandiloquent chords
From the wilderness of our sinews
Dance the denizens of mystery
Strummed the heartstrings to overtures of bliss
Strings of yearning antiquity

Awaken in that mordent cadence
Orchestrated in accord to thee
How solemnity pours with liturgical course;
Compositions of Bach and Vivaldi
I will be there, great mornings childe
To usher the gloam unto thee
Awaken here, an eternal treasure
Awaken here, with me

I put my hands over her ears and made my words flesh

The Devil's Troubadour

I am the Devil's troubadour
Lyricist of poisoned words
An arcane flame of deviltry
The tongue of pariahs accursed

I am as the songs of revolt
That reviles the sanctity of the heavenly
Along with his minstrels of witches and goats
The hymn of satanic revelry

Hitherto mine, recital of fates
Reviled in chants of broken verse
Foretold in the fold of soliloquy and song
In each tone a note, to intone the perverse

Hither to mine, aphorisms, sophisms
That confound and craft thy curse
Lies for truth and truth for lies
In each note a prayer in perfect reverse

I am the Devil's troubadour
Inimical but well versed
Illimitable by design
Precise and unrehearsed…

I poeticize blasphemy
Atop vast iniquitous hymns
I precipitate all perfidies
In sutras of splendorous sin

And while the wile tempter
I myself a bit, tendentious
Antithetical and heretical
Unapologetic and contentious

I am the diatribe in rhyme
The poet HE adores,
The antagonist of convention;
The Devil's troubadour

And with each verse the poison breeds

The words I write, the words you read...

"Behold the mathematics of chaos
And the surplus; universe
The implicate and explicate layers
Infinite and transverse

Humanity stands in neutrality
Wedged within the seams
Of the expanding fabric of reality
Unaware of what it means

6,000 years of celestial physiology
Yet a mere second away from death
The ephemeral sleep unknowingly
Of eternity undreamt and left"

Sirens of the Brine

Littoral cantabiles
Farewell, there bid thy strings
Minstrels plucking tender songs
Sending off, their royal offspring
The strums, the strings
Ye harbingers bring
Roused from the brine
Ghostly sirens sing
Lending their voices to the minstrels 'tween
Lustrous brine and lucid dream

Calling in unearthly drones
From subterranean catacombs
Down the rivulets
Of oceans cadence
Where eternities the sirens bestow

A patchwork of marvel sound
Of spells, in somnolence wove
Where the immortal dreamers dare to dream
The sleepers dare not know

Nor can they ever hear the sirens
Nor hear the gifts of the ageless sea
Dare not ask, ye temporal sleepers
Such dreams are not for thee

Nor do they feel the restless clamor
That aches as darkness sweeps
For the return of her children

As these lay sound asleep.

The obscurantists, we misdirect
From where our indolence leads
Lucid, languid but onward
To our secret, infinite dream
To the sweetest scented waters
That beckons us to venture
Past the oscillating tides of night and day
Into twilight's profoundest indenture

And the sleepers hear never the sirens
For such resonance is for we
Dare not ask, ye temporal sleepers
Such dreams are not for thee

the Hyperborean

I am theogony in prose
Hermeticist of Scythia
My powers vast and rapt
As the beauty of Cytheria

I am as that priest of Apollo
As I've the "golden arrow"
Wherewith shall I travel
Unseen, beyond the morrow

I do not eat, I do not drink
Such dire needs mean naught to me
I go as God and unredeemed
I come as yonder memory

Lo! Behold, all Trojans
Bones to Minerva
Talisman from heaven
Protector and preserver

Lo! Wondrous Pythagoras
I honed and bestowed
The gifts of invisibility
And the feats of moral gold

I've the formulas that expiate
And the "magical papyrus"
I am oracle and Magi
Or so saith Suidas

And in my might I am brighter
Then Ursa Minor about Polaris
I am "The Hyperborean"
The magician named Abaris

I pacify the tempests
And cure all disease
I presage remotest ventures
Past, present and yet to be

Past the northern shore
Aloft the oar of thee; Black Sea
Behold! The Hyperborean
Abaris, that is me!

VII

They are silenced in murmurs and disheveled with fear

Abandoned by "God" in their final quarter

Resigned with certainty, for the inevitable nears

And like proper forage, they crawl to their slaughter

Genocide in an eye,
Pogrom in my palm
The funerary dirge and the penitent psalm

How romantic comes death,
Sought after the qualm...
Death again and again

Saphomet

Courting the muses, sweetest Saphomet
Abating restrictions both imposed and made
For lovers as such, upon a whim they brush,
Both female and unashamed…
Two of one such, how gently they touch
With the passions of Lesbos aflamed

Lesbian swans, in Sappho's sweet plumage
Without need or regard for the swain
'Though immured be men's eyes with your beauty
Yearning be their loins, in pain
In still waters enrapt, in thy mesmeric trap
Entranced lay the voyeurs' awaste
Never to touch, how cursed art such
To know but yet never, to taste

Contemplations
of
Belphegor

I've ravaged and consumed
To gross surfeit and ballooned
To a round bellied beast
Idle and slothful
From the crapulence of the glut
At inertia's disposition
The existential lethargy
And the indolent prison
Whom dare disturbeth, my repose?
I am filled with the blood of Christian souls
I am tired from my labors
Chewing flesh and spitting bones
Eating souls from the scribes
…Immolated in their tomes

...Now, the following two
Are with tongue in cheek,
And after the balm,
For how sweet love can be...
And for God's sweet indifference,
Is where love can lead...
When life, is to love,
There Gods often feed.

Unto Regret,
Tumultuous Revelry

Charlatans and harlots sin
The barley lagers, filled to the brim
When consumption amounts
Refinement dims…and then we'll drink again

Fill my cup with arrogance
And plenty expletives
Fill my cup with dragging staggers
Non-sequiturs and belches

Fill my cup with hiccups
And uncoordinated dances
Fill my cup with lewd intentions
And unwarranted advances

Fill my cup with "I feel sick"
With nauseating bliss,
With "where's your lavatory?"
And "where's the man I kissed?"

Oh fill my cup with nihilism
And fill it to the brim
For I refuse to remember tomorrow night,
Today's ignominious whim

Grant Me O' Devils

Grant me oh devils'
Another man's wife
That I've none of my own
To cause me one strife
One sheltered and nurtured
Yes, one provided for
For one I never a cent
From my pocket withdraw
That I not one affection
To ever yet waste
Let affections waste they
On the smite of my taste
On this selfish shell
On the scourge of my being
Covetousness embody
Yearning and seeing
Blondes, reds, pale brunettes
Sweet scented and soft
Come one, twice, thrice aplenty
But come my dears, betrothed
Yes, grant me oh devils'
Another man' wife
A commoner's lady
Bored with her life
Conformed to the uniform,
Unvarying monotonous
Years of dull union
Depressingly monogamous
Dispirited femininity
With passions extinguished

Forsake those vows
Surrender, relinquish
This night, to arouse
From this unsullied flesh,
That dormant whore
That thou hath repressed
So, open your legs
And let - me - come - in
What he does not know
Dear, will - not - hurt - him
Oh grant me oh devils'
Another man's wife
For I come with a hunger
And I come with rife
Render them still
And offering pleasantries
My delicate pleasures, these
Adulterous delicacies
My unwavering desire
Ere wrought with much blithe
Come now, grant me o' devils',
Another man's wife

The Balm from a Godless Gland

The rod enflamed anew
As the campanile obstructing the clouds
A flesh Cathedral precipice,
Prepuce pulled back to a howl
Stiffened like rigor mortis
And ejaculating unborn death
This tower is now fallen
The servants swallowed and now repent

A Love Awry: For Amaelia

She said aloud:

Must you always say "I love you"
before "coitus" and never after?
Must you always relieve
your lust, upon my face?

And ignore the shards
of this heart that you shatter,
repeating this abuse
unto a lovers disgrace?

This spirit is broken
in callowness wreathen
and strangled by the facsimile
of a lover I've once known

Who now reciprocates
my affections in faux smiles and pose
that will degenerate to wrath
if I lose my control

He thought in silence:

Have you not tasted the last
of my soul immaculate,
with each drop of ejaculate
and purge of life?

Your lachrymal countenance
in silence replies.
What a glutton for punishment
and a sight for sore eyes.

Tears my dear, are ineffectual
when soliciting compassion
as is petitioning me for sentiments
of which, I haven't comprehension

As is courting my contention
with self-condescension and lackaday
How I despise, here and now
what I loved once yesterday

Apathy and indifference could never be evil.
For along with mute invisibility, they
are God's greatest characteristics.

This Side of Mourning; A Suicide Poem She Wrote:

My arms that shone of tiny holes
Were loneliness could see
My poisoned soul forlorn of hope
And filled with misery
        "Oh blessed childe, Oh mourning's childe",
He said:
        "Distempered thy heart, of tragedies begotten
        Come enter the garden for the end it seems,
        Is merely a dream and soon after forgotten"

Forlorn of love, light flees your breast
When darkness resides where suicides nest
I'm disavowing all hope from faith's faint breath
Should I dare breathe again, tomorrow

        "Oh tortured orchid, wilting in hand,
He said:
        Delicate in thy ghastly pallor
        Sleep deep my dear, in dream shares and ether
        As I await thee in joyous pasture"

        "Oh token childe, oh broken childe
He said:
        "Do thyself slowly, but do come trodden

        Come enter my garden
        This is painless, you'll see
        And all too soon, forgotten"

And the sun shaking off its final embers
Dims my penultimate hour
While recollections now flail,
To the peal of a bell
And a wintry wind to cower
Of family and friends…
Of lovers and regrets…
Of poets, whose lines I've borrowed -

"Sleep deep my dear
In dream shares and ether
'Til darkness enshrouds the morrow"

I've made of thee my minstrel
Now I sever twain, thy strings
I've exulted thee, - an angel
To now pull apart thy wings
And it hurts me indeed, to hurt you
But you know my dear, I must
For you deserve what you accept from me
For our actions all define us
For you deserve what you accept, you see?
My tattered doll, my angel love
Weep, ye string-less minstrel
Die, ye ravaged dove

Idling toward the Gloam

In there o' darkling, we do dwell
This side of mourning, no 'God' dispels
When the eventide looms,
For at last to resume
The prelude to splendour
Vast night and full moon

Bay the wolves, the wintry scourge
From the crypt of the flesh
To the lure of the world
In desultory, to roam
Idling t'ward the gloam
Guided by voices, leading us home

Dolce Penumbra

Violin of the tenebrous hour,
Your melodies aggrieve
The hymns of burdensome mantra
And baroque novelty
Imbibe its ceaseless detriment,
Death sings upon the breeze
For her rhapsody of mourning,
Shall be, one day, for thee
Cotillion of grand misfortune,
Wisp of anguished delights
Play thy horrid languor,
'Tis time to claim a life

To my vengeful machinations,
I should be loath to deny

Animosity with apathy,
An eye for an eye

the Witching Hour

Dawn of the witching
To claim a soul they're bating
O'er wroth and callous craving
- To cast a feast, in Hell's deep sating
Oh, the coals of curses making
In the brass braziers there baking
The frankincense perfuming
The gong struck, the silence breaking
Unsheathed my sword, un-girding
Amid the akashic stirring
Effervesced, the chalices blood
In with trembled words incurring
And thunder, as patterned to my heart
Come crashing and obeying
Oh death in cauldrons burning
The hours of judgment weighing

When the walls become liquid, the poetry flows…

The aeonian font where the muses repose

"The auspices of a vague nuance, vaguer than these
lines I conceive
Mademoiselle obfuscate, there is magic in subtlety
Mademoiselle run with the winds, and hide amidst
the trees
But first dear mademoiselle, undress and lie with me"

Whispering LaVoison

Thou hath, as wicked Sybil
Bewitched my hearts abode
Incessant in thy wickedness
Imprecations thy spell unwove

'Tis thy love, that taketh me there
Your kiss of bite, your thrusts of sting
And the moans of euphonious rapture
Like fallen Seraphim sing:

My dear love! My dear love!
My souls breadth is deeply snared
From the raffish, chimerical grin
To the garters coquettishly bared

My dear love! To taste a breath so fair
Of antique rose and cognac
Drunk and rendered bare
To a pale chartreuse and lilac
That immured my mirrored glare
Jaundiced with lips of purplish death

In the chemical scented air

Wreathen in the undertow
Of liquid clouds and starry mist
Whispering: "my dear LaVoison",
Beneath the embalmers kiss
And to memories of ye, my love
Did I in this poison swim
My soul, as in a deep hallucinogen
'Til consciousness their dimmed

…Whilst a dream of broken fishnets
Beneath a coat of leopard print,
Bestrode an illusion of mystic glamour
To my frenzied heart, bewitched

- Evoked 'neath the embalmers kiss
For under her spell I stood
As no swoon nor paregoric bliss
Was ever quite as good

- Rendering me a moment of thee
This strange epiphany upon a wing
In a choir of screeching caterwauls
Bad luck, the black cats sing:

My dear love! My dear love!
- Awakened from such bliss
Having heard "My dear LaVoison"
Beneath the embalmers kiss

Rapid eye movements and the lyceum of the mind...

Empyrean fields of angels conspiring against God...

Testimonial of Cain

Igneous thought
With a scintillant urge
Evil suggested
To which I concurred
Ridden with un-implorable
And impetuous silence
Stolid in the afterglow
Of my truncheon purge,
Lo! Ghost of God
Hear now my confession!
With ribald glibness
In derelict rendition,
In tawdry stance
With guiltless conviction,
Inscrutably vile
I emphatically reveal
The blood of my wanton
And ever rifling zeal

In profoundest remote
'Neath shaded green veil,
I lifted a stone
And forward, assailed.
Your cherished little Abel
Did not see the blow…

But running red rivers
And trembling death throes.
Oh brother dear brother,
I wish you to know,

I did not hate thee
But loved greater God's woe
" If thou didst offer well
But divide badly hast,
Thou not committed sin? "
- His eminence asked
Ungrateful swine
This God malign
How dare ye reject
This oblation of mine
I would kill a thousand Abels
To see you weep
Impetuous Lord
Castigating mere sheep
" Where is your brother Abel? "
- Am I my brother's keeper?
If thou art omniscient
-Why inquire? Peer deeper.
Does the blood of my brother
Cry out from the earth?
I unmercifully retorted
For what it is worth

And so "condemned" was I
To eternal strife;

Exiled from God
And confined to night
Unbeknownst of the consequence
Spawned of my action -
I'd have killed him much sooner
With greater satisfaction

So hearken oh Lord
Creator, "All Mighty"
Insecure bore
Trite demander of piety
I'd murder them all
Every beast on this land
Every plant that uproots
From the design of your hand
All things that live,
That fly, crawl or scrimmage
All things that bear
A semblance of thine image
So hear my confession
And do as thou wilt
Every crimson transgression
Every death that is dealt
I confess to it all
And repent not a word
But multiply thy provocation
'Til your stomach is stirred
'Til you cough and retch
The bile of your firmament
For in sin do I letch
For your angel's lament

So reap the sufferance
That sows my contempt
That knows no respite
In spite o' all that is pent
So choke on my words
And quaff this disdain
I confess to it all,

As I relish your pain -
I confess to it all
As I sign here my name
With the blood of dead Abel
Sincerely,
- Lord Cain

Vas Maledictum

In the gruesome it looms

Rapacious and ravenous

To inseminate every crevice

With the seedlings of sacrilege

And pollinate thy womb

With the flume of its egress

By the terrors of the mind

And the tortures of the flesh

In the gruesome it looms

Virile and venomous

Ever stalking its prey

Esurient and carnivorous

Insatiable its thirst,

'Though it consumes in excess

No indulgence will assuage

No denial will suppress

In the gruesome it looms

By the wicked extolled

Repulsing the mind

Disgusting the soul

And at a moments un-notice

Shall rage forth, at a whim

The evils that bind

Lurking within

Mute Judas Sings

Mute I clamor, with this kiss
Catalyst bridge betwixt:
The sins of my lips
And the riches I have wished
Mute I clamor, with this
A kiss of indemnity to false providence
Redolent of treason, indulgence, indifference
Mute I clamor: CRUCIFY HIM!
And enter ye Romans; ushers of the damned

The Lineaments Lugubrious

I can smell it happening.
The world's "oldest profession"
The lineaments lugubrious
Looming, without discretion
And there, the stranger and the dealer
Discussing a cost to ease
Life's detriment and sentiments,
Body lice and disease

From rabid meows of froth and foam
Past empty vials on cobblestones
I can feel them squirming
Through penitence, through broken homes
Through addiction's pungent stench
Through trails of trash and bone
Lined track marks the needles prick
The lineaments lugubrious
- Anointing of the sick

…with a fiendish grin he drunkenly neared,
those despicable lips dare whispered my ear:

'DeLana

"Her powdered nose and maquillage
Enhance a gentle face
A porcelain doll with perfect smile
Precocious yet scarcely aged
With quaint to whimsical badinage
Her candor is displayed
A poetess of polemics
With quotes from every sage
And down her silken décolletage
An ample bust is gauged
What breasts I ought to fondle
What mouth I ought to rape"

Listen in darkness
                    The whistling winds

The hiss of snakes
                    In Christian sins

The balm drops down the foulest swallow
Savor its venom tonight and tomorrow
There is no protection from the snares of corruption
Not in these lairs, not of this gumption
So waiver your souls in sin old consumption
'Til death and Hell that follows

Dreams in Exodus:

ODE TO DEATH ON A JUNKIE

Dreams in exodus, intravenous nirvana
Foreclosed in dolorous slumber
Fled ye, all too soon
To the merciless scourge of morning
That blasted bright the room;
The sun's luminous plunder
With punishment resumes.
In thy pallor and frailty
And shuddering squints,
Cold sweats and stomachal fits,
The wretched countenance from atrophy lifts
To the scenting fumes of a summertime dew
And the dainty dreadfuls of addiction

Inhabit here the squalor
And with psoriasis indulge
Your cracking thin blue lips
On a tawdry stranger's bulge
For a dainty dirty syringe
Therein thine stringent dole
Beauty; the wasted brokenness
Your eyes my dear, divulge
And oh, how lovely the wretched weep
From desertion and grieving sorrow
But back on the streets as nature deems
'Til death and Hell that follows

O' junkie whore of dastard chores
If for a fix then fixed on fours
So lick your lips
And taste those sores
Of gonococcus trysts and venereal spores
Be off, come again
And in thy arms new bores
Nights knelt working, -Days, praying to implore
Mercy, misericord, an end to it all…
But in thy pallor and frailty
And muttering quips
Cramped limbs, jaundiced skin
And pants filled with shit
If for a fix you insist, you'd either spit or swallow?
Then childe on your knees - as nature deems
'Til death and Hell that follows

(Once in sleeping reverie...)

I will speak of morals
Entrenched in another man.
In his blood, in his ass,
Before his wife, on his land.
For naught shall dictate me
But the predilections of my hand

An Elegy to Religion

O' Holy Spirit, from my soul
I solemnly recant
Of Gods'- forlorn and Christ's'- bereft
Ingest such lies, I shan't
I have wretched my soul free from indoctrination:
The remnants of idolatry
And the revenant of God
I repudiate these abstractions of man,
His love of ghosts
In cathedral facades
Faith; a layman's fervor, impassioned by senility
How foolish the enamored,
What simpleton credulity!
I renounce "the Holy ghost", "the Father and the Son"
Replaced this, aged trinity
With: I, Myself and Me
I have expunged your gospels, your ten commands
Your divine pretense;
Earthen fallacy
The songs that herd you, slave-flocks of sheep
The words of programmed servility

Sit, stand, kneel,
What blatant puppetry
Do you fetch and roll over?
Will you beg? Do you squeal?

…The insipid alone mimic godliness,
Whose dead heavens recompense
The lie of God takes precedence

The closer one comes to death
But your doctrine and diction your dogma of fiction
…Mere traditions imposing their binds
"Ye must have faith!
Ye must have faith!"
- The vulgar parlance of incurable minds

Love; Laconic and Terse

I will appropriate my love to truth
And abscond my ways from gallantry
Why should an animal's tongue
Be demoted to propriety?
For I am free and I am beast
And I lust with inhumane voracity
For instincts are and will always see
Action defy morality

The flaccid linguists of love;
A shorn and shrewd, contemptible brood
Of celibate hands and eunuch tools
- Cure her of this, wonder of fools
From the antics of Cupid's
Arrows and bows
To the pedantic semantics
In poetry and prose
- Lust has replaced love
Or did you not know?
Eden is sullen, barren and abandoned
Behold a new paradise…
Within the flames

Immaculate duality
Like Hermes and Aphrodite
Until our evils engender
With our sordid lusting bodies
Prostrated before desire
Wretched and immersed in bliss
Will we sever?
Will it not,
For such should lust persist

'Camphor Dune Tansy'

Creation's wisp, the beginning of an organism
Blooming like camphor dune tansy
Of an exotic minority, woven vines
With the wildest rose, romancing

Feign me here, a sweetest innocence
Like a virgin violet upon a wild pansy
For a moment endeared, I will quaff the pretense
Dainty like camphor dune tansy

As I mock my knowing, for a futile gift;
The lie of love and a lover's frenzy
Like cherubs tonight; we gently tryst
In a garden of camphor dune tansy

The habitual self is always stronger than the ideal model

Carnalia, New York:

"TENDERLOIN CHELSEA"

Harem of serpentines
Purify our flesh once more with dances
Tongues roving, wandering
The salient citadels
Rabid with desire
And sweat filled shells
Fellating each other like mad cannibals
The passion laden crevices and saccharine clefts,
Burning loins and pendulous breasts
Our spirits condemned to our bodies duress
Press upon and quell

Until temptation insists
Unto temptation subside
These panderers may connive
But these panderers provide
Now back in the saloon, engaged to forget
Gambling with mavericks and collecting all debts
Where the beasts in blood
Bathe and repose
How sickly and vitiated…
The place I call home

The drunkard cant bleating ho-hum
Skid rows and the metropolis slum
Red light district beneath a blood red sun
Wine and women, which I remember none

Now back in the brothel, without a regret
Slithering with serpentines, writhing in a bed
Where the beasts in blood
Bathe and repose
How sickly and vitiated…
The place I call home

I am NOT a "rebel"
For rebellion is the cry of the oppressed
I my dear, am the oppressor
And I offer you duress

I spied the buxom, crimson haired bride
Dispossessed in constant sigh
Lit up her smoke as I looked up her thigh
Leaned in for a kiss but she started to cry.
As she whispered to me, so eerily
"T'was a night like this… that you died."

In the arms of your angels, may you now flee from here.

the Serpent

Suffer my citation
Whose enamored vassals behold my glory
Slithering into Eden
To persuade thee into knowing,
To envenom thee listless
My pale and naked quarry
I am the serpentine tongue of the Gods
Uncoiled and ever whoring

Nomenon MoriVond

Through uncharted lands,
Un-trodden sands
Through mausoleums of shun prophecy
Abroad moribund terrain
I have manifested as Thy litany
In the caverns of the desolate,
In the solace of sovereignty
And eternities at Thy behest

Mother night and fertile whore,
Bare me such barbarous delights.
My body is a temple, wherein all demons reside;
A pantheon of flesh am I.
My ecumenical council; the birds of prey
My masses; the forests. My altar; the earth
I shall hold rites and masses of wine and promiscuous dances,
Let them pay homage with sacrilege
And paeans of thunder

I am the tongue and the tale of the Dragon
Whom none should assume to fathom
- the slithering truth
That precedes the fruit
Persuading the Eve and the Adam
- the slithering truth
That pervades today,
The ancient hymn, whose sins serenade,
The sum of great tribulation
And the coming end of days
I have journeyed the farthest reaches

Assailed aeons of perilous night
Bewailed my heart in thine oblation
And bled dry my sacrifice
Enterin Great Lourds! Effulgent Undead
My heart bleeds of fealty
Partake of its ebb
For such resounds its beating litany
That roused the oceans depths
I have died
I am risen
I will come again…

About the Author

Self –proclaimed "American Heretic", outspoken libertine and admirer of the Romantic and Decadent aesthetes of the 18th and 19th centuries, MoriVond tends to incorporate an extravagant, archaic tone to a catalogue of perverted musings and hallucinatory abstraction.

This is the author's first authorized collection of published works.

For more information visit www.devilstroubadour.com

Made in the USA
Coppell, TX
16 August 2024